My Worst Day...
And How I Survived It

Edited by Sarah Verney and Naomi Kirsten

Discovery Girls, Inc.

CALIFORNIA

Discovery Girls, Inc.
445 South San Antonio Rd, Ste. 205
Los Altos, California 94022

My Worst Day...And How I Survived It

All of the stories in this collection were originally published in *Discovery Girls* magazine between December 2000 and August 2009. Some stories have been edited or revised for inclusion in this collection. "Diabetes Changed My Whole Life," was originally published as "Living With Diabetes," "Drugs Changed My Cousin's Life Forever" was originally published as "A Cousin in Crisis," "I'm Not Stupid" was originally published as "Learning to Live With Learning Disabilities," "I Toilet-Papered My Teacher's House" was originally published as "I Was in So Much Trouble," "It's Hard to Be the New Girl" was originally pusblished as "School Daze," "My BFF Totally Rejected Me" was originally published as "A False Friendship," "My Broken Family" was originally published as "Divorce Is...Never Easy," "My Stepdad Doesn't Love Me" was originally published as "My Stepdad Doesn't Love Me Anymore," "My Mom Died" was originally published as "The Long Goodbye," and "Robbed at Gunpoint" was originally published as "Living in Fear." Unless otherwise noted, all poll results are from 2012 DiscoveryGirls.com.

ISBN 978-1-934766-07-1

Visit Discovery Girls' web site at DiscoveryGirls.com.

Printed in the United States of America.

Dedication

Dedicated to the thousands of girls who have taken the time to write to *Discovery Girls* magazine to share your ideas, thoughts, personal stories, and yes, even your problems. All of us who work at Discovery Girls, Inc. have been deeply touched by your letters. You are a constant source of insight and inspiration, and the reason we have created this book.

Acknowledgments

I'd like to send a special thank you to all the girls who have read *Discovery Girls* magazine over the years and have generously shared your thoughts, ideas, and experiences with us. Without you, there would be no *Discovery Girls* magazine and definitely no Discovery Girls books. I feel so very lucky to have had the opportunity to work with my dedicated and talented staff: Julia Clause, Ashley DeGree, Naomi Kirsten, Katherine Inouye Lau, Alex Saymo, Bill Tsukuda, Sarah Verney, and interns Lyn Mehe'ula, Laura Riparbelli, and Nick Tran. Your enthusiasm and ability to keep your sense of humor while meeting insane deadlines, your willingness to work long hours, your amazing creative energy, and your insistence on always striving to get better and better have meant more to me than you will ever know—my deepest appreciation!

Catherine Lee
PUBLISHER
DISCOVERY GIRLS, INC.

Contents

My ⛈ Worst Day

...and How I Survived It

An 11-year-old girl and her mom are sitting in their car when a man thrusts a gun in the window and grabs the mom's purse. The girl isn't hurt, but for months afterward she doesn't want to leave her house...for anything. A popular straight-A student is so mad at her newly-divorced parents that she gains 20 pounds, pushes her friends away, and starts getting D's. A girl loses all her friends in one day after two boys play a mean trick on her. The teacher's pet "honors" the teacher she adores by draping her house and yard in toilet paper...and ends up in deep trouble.

Tough times? You bet. Some of these stories are sad enough to bring tears to your eyes, and some might make you so angry you want to scream. But you'll find tons of encouragement here, too. Because as different as these stories are, there's something they all have in common: In every one, the girl walks away stronger, smarter, and more sure of herself than she's ever been before.

You can read these stories for comfort, for inspiration, or just to see how someone else handled a problem you're dealing with. They'll help you see that—no matter what you're going through—you're not alone. You'll meet girls who are so much like you, you'll feel like you know them. And by the last page, you'll have a whole new way of looking at bad days and tough times!

—The Editors of *Discovery Girls*

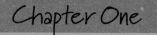

Chapter One

WHEN YOU DON'T FIT IN

All My Friends Left Me!

By Lauren-Kristine, age 12, Texas

*I*N MY SCHOOL, THE CLIQUES HAVE ALL been together since kindergarten. You joined a group, and that was that. That never used to bother me because I had my friends—especially my two best friends, Caitlin and Katy, who were always there for me. I *did* have other friends, just not close ones. Being friends with Katy and Caitlin was enough.

And then it all fell apart. We were sitting on the sidelines of our basketball game when Caitlin suddenly exclaimed, "Guess what?" "What?" I replied, expecting a surprise. Instead she said, "I'm moving."

"My best friends would be thousands of miles away by the end of June."

"You're joking, right?" I said, praying that it *was* just a big joke. "No," Caitlin replied, her face tense. "I'm not. I'm moving to Qatar, near Saudi Arabia. My dad's been transferred there for the next two years."

I stared at her in disbelief, and then started to cry. Caitlin couldn't move away! What would I do without her?

Miles Away

It got worse. A few days later I found out that Katy was also moving—to Australia! *Both* of my best friends would be thousands of miles away by the end of June. It was like I was a chalkboard and my friendships with Katy and Caitlin were being erased. Years of work on our friendship were gone in an instant.

I know it was hard on both Katy and Caitlin, too. They had to leave their school, their friends—*everything*—and get used to new people and new places. I felt bad for them, but at least *they* were both going off on adventures. *I* was just going to be stuck at home with no friends. I couldn't help it—I felt sorriest of all for *me*.

"It was awful. Everyone had a group to hang out with— except me."

Saying goodbye to Katy and Caitlin was very hard, just as I'd expected. But the summer wasn't as lonely as I'd thought it would be. I still had my not-so-close friends, so I wasn't totally on my own. Still, I really missed having my best friends around. I couldn't wait for school to start again—I kept hoping like crazy that there would be some new fifth grade girls that I could make friends with.

Ignored

But there wasn't even one new girl that year! It was just the same old cliques, except now I was completely on the outside.

It was awful. Everyone had a group to hang out with except me. At least if I'd been new, some kids would have been curious about me, or they'd have been friendly because I *was* new. But since everyone already knew me, they just ignored me.

I went home every night and cried. I felt so rejected! I tried hard to be really friendly and nice to everyone, but nothing seemed to get better. In fact, the harder I tried to fit in, the more the popular kids teased me and called me a loner. And as the weeks went by, I started to think that they were right, and I was going to be stuck being a "loner" until I started middle school the next year. But finally my mom reminded me of someone I'd overlooked.

> "I went home every night and cried. I felt so rejected!"

Taking a Chance

I'd known Jill since first grade, and I'd always liked her, even though we weren't super close friends. Not only was she really nice, I realized *she* could probably use a best friend, too, since she'd been having a lot of trouble with her old "best" friends. She wasn't part of the popular group, and I knew she wouldn't put me down for trying to be friends with her. I decided to give it a shot.

I started hanging out with Jill every day at recess, and talking to her whenever we ran into each other. Then I invited her to spend the night at my house a couple of times. Suddenly our friendship started to blossom. Pretty soon our casual conversations turned into deep conversations. We talked about *everything*—and suddenly a new piece of chalk started drawing on that chalkboard! I stopped dreading school and felt wanted and liked again.

IT'S BEEN OVER A YEAR NOW SINCE CAITLIN AND KATY moved away, but we're still really close. Caitlin visited me this summer, and we even went to sleep-away camp together. And Katy is thinking about visiting in December! I still wish they hadn't had to move, but I also realize that there *have* been some good things about this experience. I feel more confident now about my ability to make friends. I've also learned how to ignore teasing and believe in myself, and how to stay optimistic. I have definitely become stronger emotionally and spiritually.

Now I have *three* best friends—two far away, and one close by, who gives me a lift every day!

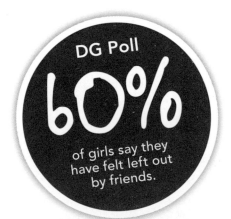

DG Poll

60%

of girls say they have felt left out by friends.

"Because I liked to sing and perform, I was an outsider."

I Was Bullied

By Callie, age 12, Ohio

H

AVE YOU EVER BEEN BULLIED?
I have, and it was terrifying. I got headaches that hurt so much I'd get sick to my stomach. My doctor thought I might have a brain tumor. But after he did a bunch of tests, he had a different diagnosis: extreme stress.

How can a 12-year-old girl have so much stress? For two years, a group of kids in my school picked on me *constantly*. They pushed me around and laughed at me. They called me names, tripped me, and put nasty notes in my locker. One time, a girl even threw my jacket into the toilet.

It started after I'd been chosen to be in a children's chorus in Cleveland. I got to perform with other kids in a huge concert. The performance was broadcast on TV. My picture was in the newspaper, so even though I never talked about it at school, kids knew. After that weekend, one girl said to me, "You think you're so popular!"

> "They called me names, tripped me, and put nasty notes in my locker."

Jealous?

That hurt, but it confused me, too. I had friends, but I'd never thought of myself as "so popular," because I *wasn't*. When I got home, I asked my mom what she meant. My mom said she was probably just jealous. My parents had always told me I shouldn't talk about performing when I was at school—not because I shouldn't be proud of my accomplishments, but because kids might think I was bragging. I was beginning to understand what my parents meant.

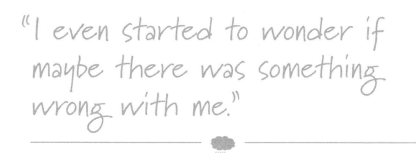

"I even started to wonder if maybe there was something wrong with me."

An Outsider

From then on, it got worse at my Catholic school. Most of the girls did sports and Girl Scouts, but because I liked to sing and perform, I did different activities, which made me an outsider.

When I tried to tell my teachers and the principal what was going on, they didn't believe me. My parents *did* believe me, though. They talked to my teacher, the school counselor, and principal, too. But my teacher was also the softball coach, and most of the bullies were on her team. She couldn't believe that her girls, who were from "good Catholic families," would ever mistreat anyone.

Rejection

I think I'm a pretty strong person. If you want to perform, you have to face rejection. You audition a lot and you get turned down for all sorts of reasons. You get rejected because your hair is the wrong color or you're too tall or too short or because of something else you can't control. But whatever it is, it's always about the work. It isn't really about *you* as a person.

It's different—and so hurtful—when you're being cut down by your classmates just for being yourself. I started to wonder if maybe they were right, that there *was* something wrong with me. I felt so alone.

"I realized all that bullying was about them, not me."

The summer after sixth grade, I went to camp with other kids. I traveled a lot, performed in dance competitions, and got to hang out with my friends. I stopped being so stressed and my headaches went away.

A New School

I decided I *really* wanted to switch to the public school. My parents didn't agree, so I set out to convince them. I interviewed public school kids in my neighborhood and made a list of all the reasons public school would be better for me. I put the school's no tolerance policy toward bullying at the top.

It took a while to convince my parents, but they finally agreed with me. Even though my new school was big and scary at first, it was 10 times better than my old school. By October I'd made a bunch of new friends. Still, the bullying didn't end! The kids from my old school rode a bus that stopped at the public school every day, and whenever I walked by, they'd yell rude things at me.

One day a guidance counselor from my new school saw this and put a stop to it. But even if he hadn't, the teasing no longer got to me like it used to. Believe it or not, I felt sorry for the bullies now. Remember what I said about how being rejected at an audition doesn't hurt so much because it's not about you? I finally realized that all that bullying wasn't about me, either. Those kids picked on me because there was something wrong with *them,* not me. They're mean, unhappy people, and that's just sad.

I ALSO LEARNED THAT I HAVE THE COURAGE TO GO AFTER THE things I want. Last year, I auditioned for a role in an off-Broadway production of "A Christmas Carol"—and I got it! You know what the best part was, though? I've got great new friends, and they were totally supportive and truly happy for me. It just doesn't get any better than that.

DG Poll

32%

of girls say they've been seriously bullied.

I Thought I Was Ugly

By Alexis,* age 12, Ill.

I HATE MYSELF, *I* HATE MYSELF, *I* HATE myself! I was lying in bed, trying to sleep, but I couldn't make those thoughts stop. Finally, I grabbed my diary and wrote:

> *Dear Diary,*
> *Today I was drawing a picture of myself when my*
> *so-called friend Mattie walked by and whispered to*
> *Lizzie, "Wow, that looks almost as weird as she is in*
> *person." Is it true? Do I really look weird? I know I'm*
> *not as skinny as these girls, and my hair isn't perfectly*
> *straight or all curly and pretty. Maybe I AM weird.*
> *I feel like an elephant next to toothpicks! I never*
> *want to go to school again! EVER!*
>
> *Yours,*
> *Alexis*

I drew another picture of myself, based on what I felt like I saw in the mirror. I gave myself super frizzy hair, a round pot belly, a shirt with "unpopular" written on it, and big clown shoes. Then I threw my diary on the floor and finally fell asleep.

Mom Reads My Diary

A little while later, my mom came in to my room to say goodnight and saw my diary. Since I'd never left it lying around before, she wondered if maybe I'd *meant* for her to read it...so she did. She saw my "self-portrait," and it really worried her.

The next day my mom told me that she'd read my diary. At first all I could think was, *How could you invade my privacy like that?!* But I calmed down when she told me how concerned she was. Truthfully, as mad as I was, I was also a little glad. It felt good to let it all out. I was tired of always wishing I looked more like the popular girls, and tired of worrying that I would never measure up.

My mom had recently seen something on *Oprah* about moms, daughters, and low self-esteem, so she wrote Oprah a letter about what I'd written in my diary. She even sent her a copy of my self-portrait. Maybe if they'd talk about girls like me, there would be some information on the show that would help my mom help me.

"Oprah wanted me to be on her show! We were shocked!"

Oprah to the Rescue

About a week later, Harpo Studios (Oprah's company) called my mom. They'd read my mom's letter, and they wanted me to be on the show. My mom and I were shocked! I was feeling a million things at once: Going on TV sounded really exciting, but I was also terrified. Everyone who watched would know what I'd written in my diary. I already felt my entire school thought I was ugly. Now the whole country would see me. Did I really want that?

My mom and I talked about it and finally I decided to go through with it. The day of the show, as I waited for my turn to go on, they showed the picture I'd drawn. Seeing it up on the screen and knowing all the people in the audience were looking at it was really embarrassing. I could hardly breathe.

Then I went onstage and Oprah asked me some questions about what had been going through my mind when I'd drawn the picture. I answered her as honestly as I could. At the end she said, "Alexis, you are beautiful." For just a second, I couldn't catch my breath. My parents told me that all the time, but this was different. It was a powerful moment, and it gave me such a good feeling inside.

A Realization

After that, I started to think differently about what it means to be beautiful. Sure, *everyone* wants to look good. But I also think it's *more* important to worry about what's *inside* you, too, because that's what really counts—that's what makes you truly beautiful.

I know, you've heard that before. Me, too. But for some reason, after all this happened, it made sense to me in a way that it never did before. I started to really believe it. Maybe that's because I realized something else after Oprah said that I was beautiful. I realized that I had a choice.

"It was a powerful moment, and it gave me such a good feeling inside."

The Same Me

Oprah saw me one way, and Mattie saw me another way, but it was the same me standing there both times. If I let myself feel ugly when Mattie makes a mean comment, and pretty when someone else says I'm beautiful, I'm just letting *everyone else* tell me what I should think of myself. I'm just accepting someone else's opinion of me instead of deciding for myself who I really am.

Since that day, I've decided I won't let someone else tell me how to feel about myself. I want that feeling of being beautiful to come from someplace strong inside me. For me, that means accepting myself as God made me, and worrying more about what's on the inside than the outside. When people look at me now, I hope they see a unique, creative, kind girl with curly red hair and a friendly smile. Now *that's* beautiful to me!

DG Poll

50%

of girls say they don't like the way they look.

Chapter Two

FRIENDSHIP TROUBLES

My BFF Totally Rejected Me

By Aubrie, age 12, Calif.

Ashley* and I weren't just pals

that hung together as part of a clique—we were joined at the heart. You know what it's like: You share your deepest secrets and vow to stay friends forever and ever...*that* kind of friend. I had other friends, of course, but there was no one like Ashley, and I was pretty sure there never would be.

In elementary school, some girls cared way too much about what clothes they wore and which clique they should hang out with, but Ashley was never like that. She saw who people really were on the inside. She was the most loyal friend you'd ever want.

> "Imagine saying good morning to your mom without being able to move your lips."

Facioscapulohumeral...

I have a physical disability called (get ready—this is a mouthful!) Facioscapulohumeral muscular dystrophy, or FSHD. Imagine waking up in the morning and not being able to lift your head off your pillow. Or rolling out of bed and struggling to stand up. Imagine saying good morning to your mom without being able to move your lips, or trying to brush your teeth without being able to lift your hand to your mouth. FSHD is a constant challenge. It robs many of my muscles of the

*Name has been changed.

strength that most people take for granted. Because of FSHD, I have trouble walking very far, so I use a motorized scooter to get around.

But in a weird way, FSHD can also be a gift. I often have to find creative ways to solve problems instead of just going for the obvious ones. (How would you put your sweater on if you couldn't raise your arms over your head?) It's taught me to look at things from all angles, and to appreciate the powers of the imagination. I don't see my FSHD as a disability; it's just part of who I am. And when we were in grade school, that's all my FSHD was to Ashley, too. She had nothing but scorn for anyone who treated me differently because of it.

"Even though I missed Ashley terribly, I barely recognized her when she was with this new clique."

Hurt and Confused

But when we got to middle school, something changed. And that's when it happened: Ashley started to avoid me. If I took even one step in her direction, she'd dash off, tossing an excuse over her shoulder. If I said hello in the hall, she wouldn't meet my eyes. She always seemed to be running off to join a group of girls I'd hardly ever seen before. I'd watch them from a distance, feeling so alone. There was an awful, empty ache in my heart. My "forever friend" was...gone.

Even though I missed Ashley terribly, I barely recognized her when she was with this new clique. She seemed like she'd lost her confidence, and become a giggling, insecure gossip. But as much as I hated to admit it, even to myself, I was also jealous of her new friends. She'd chosen them over me.

The Truth Comes Out

After a few weeks, Ashley began to spend a little more time around me, and I allowed myself to hope that she might still want to be friends. But whenever I invited her over or did something else to try to patch things up, she'd back away again. I was so confused! Then one day she told me flat-out that she just didn't want to be friends anymore. "You look weird," she snapped. "People will think I'm weird just for being around you."

"You don't hurt someone you care about, just because you're afraid of what people might think of you."

Even When It Hurts

That's when I knew we'd never be best friends again. I'd always thought of Ashley as someone who was too strong and confident to get sucked in by the whole middle school scene. But I was wrong—really wrong. It's one thing to say or do the right thing when it doesn't cost you anything. But if you're *really* strong, you hang in there even when it's so hard it hurts. You don't hurt someone you supposedly care about, just because you're afraid of what people might think of *you*.

Finally I let Ashley go. Once I did, I was able to move on and find new best friends. It wasn't easy, of course. Good friends don't just materialize out of thin air, and I couldn't help but be cautious. But when I did let myself open up, I found friends who really do stick by me, no matter what. They're everything you could want in a friend—understanding, funny, and warm—and I treasure our friendships.

IT WOULD BE REALLY EASY TO JUST SAY THAT ASHLEY WAS weak and wrong because...well, if you ask me, she was. But it's also true that if the need to be popular can make a girl like Ashley dump her best friend, there's something wrong with the whole "system." We let the pressure to be popular have way too much power over us. Looks shouldn't matter in a friendship, and neither should popularity. If there were more girls like the friends I have now—girls confident enough not to care if someone else calls them weird—maybe we could all just be ourselves. Wouldn't that be cool?

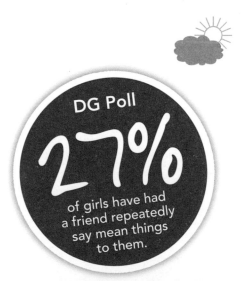

DG Poll

27%

of girls have had
a friend repeatedly
say mean things
to them.

"It was as if they had followed me home, the one place where I felt safe."

I Was Cyberbullied

By Tashana, age 13, Ontario

"Tashana is a LOSER."
"Her real name is Zit Zilla."

IT FELT LIKE I'D BEEN KICKED IN THE
stomach. My friend Ana* had called to tell me to check out a
web site. She'd said it was bad, but I still hadn't expected *this*.
Wasn't it enough that the popular kids tortured me at school?
Now it was as if they had followed me home, the one place
where I felt safe. Those words were on the Internet, where my
whole school could see them...where the whole *world* could see
them! I was totally humiliated...

When we moved earlier that year, I'd thought being "the new
girl" would be exciting. Sure, I knew I'd miss my old friends,
but I didn't think making new friends would be a problem.
I'm very outgoing, and I was sure I'd get in with a fun group.

"Seventh grade might even be my best year ever."

A New Friend
The first day, a girl named Cameron introduced herself, and
by the end of the day, I was part of her group. They reminded
me of my friends back home, always laughing and having fun,
and I felt comfortable with them. For the first few weeks, I
thought that this would be my best year ever.

*All names, except the author's, have been changed.

It wasn't perfect, though. I noticed that some things were different at this school—very different. At my old school, we didn't really have popular and unpopular cliques. People liked you for who you were, not because you hung out with the "right" people. But at this school, popularity was everything. People treated Cameron like a queen, following her around and hanging onto every word she said.

I Was Different, But...

Even though I hung out with them, I knew I was different. They all looked perfect, with beautiful skin and hair, and they all wore the latest styles. And me—well, I'm not perfect like that, but I didn't think it mattered. I thought Cameron liked me for the same reasons I liked her—because she was fun to hang out with and seemed like a loyal friend.

"I felt so alone, and I was afraid I'd be even more alone if I spoke up."

Before long, I realized that we were different in another way. Cameron and her friends were always laughing, but sometimes they were laughing *at* people. They liked making fun of people's clothes, or their looks, or even their religion! I didn't like it, but I didn't want to lose my new friends, so for a while I just let it go.

Enough!

Then one day Cameron and her friends were teasing this girl Ana, saying things like, "She's so skinny that no one can even see her!" I got mad and said, "Why do you guys think it's funny to put people down like that? It's so not cool!"

Later that day I walked into a classroom and heard a group of the popular kids whispering and laughing. "Look at Zit Zilla," one of them said. Then I heard "Pimple Face...Fish Head..." And they were talking about *me*! The whole class was looking at me and laughing—all except Ana and her friend Molly. All of a sudden, I felt sick. I wanted to run away, but I forced myself to sit at my desk and pretend there was nothing wrong. *Don't cry*, I told myself. *Just don't cry.*

"The popular kids all called me names and gossiped about me constantly."

Scared Silent

Just like that, I went from being Cameron's friend to her enemy. The popular kids all called me names and gossiped about me constantly. They played tricks on me, and sometimes when they passed me in the hall, they'd shove me into the lockers. It got so bad, I hated going to school. Every afternoon, I'd sit in my room and cry.

I wanted to just tell on them, but I was afraid. Sure, I'd get them in a little trouble—but then, wouldn't they do something even worse to me? Besides, although I knew that what Cameron and her friends were doing was wrong, part of me kept thinking that maybe the problem was *me*. Maybe I was a loser. I felt so alone, and I was afraid I'd be even *more* alone if I spoke up.

Taking Control

Then I saw the web site, and I couldn't stand it anymore. I talked to my parents. And the next day, I told the principal everything.

Since then, I've learned that I wasn't alone. A lot of kids are victims of bullies, and a lot of girls, especially, are victims of "cyberbullies." Some kids find it easy to insult someone online, because you can cut her down and never even have to see the hurt on her face. You can post embarrassing pictures or insults without admitting that you're the one doing it. For the victim, it's as bad as being bullied in person, or maybe even worse. The bullies can get you even when you're at home, in your own room, where you should feel safe.

I STARTED SPEAKING OUT ABOUT BULLYING AT MY SCHOOL and in my community. At first, it was really hard to tell my story. But instead of telling me I'm a loser, kids told me I was brave. Some people have even called me a hero!

I'm doing all I can to stop bullying. Think about it: Are you?

DG Poll

28%

of girls say they've received an insulting email, IM, or text message.

It's Hard to Be "The New Girl"

By Hannah, age 12, Fla.

Y

OU'VE PROBABLY READ THE SAME STORIES I have about being the "new girl" in school. The girl has trouble for the first day or so—maybe even the first week—but by the book's end, she not only has friends, she's popular! I believed the stories, too. Then last year, my family moved, so *I was* that new kid. I had to say goodbye to all of my friends and the place I'd lived since kindergarten. I couldn't think of anything worse.

Still, I convinced myself that going to a new school would be a *good* thing. I was sure I'd make new friends. Everyone would want to be nice to the new girl...right?

"I convinced myself that going to a new school would be a good thing."

First Day

As I walked into school on the first day, my heart was pounding. Kids were all around me, hugging each other and squealing. No one seemed to notice me. I made my way alone through the tight knots of people, telling myself that this was typical first-day-of-school stuff. *They'll have time for me later*, I thought.

At lunch, most people were sitting in small cliques, so I sat down alone. When some kids invited me to sit with them, I was so relieved. Even though we didn't talk, I still felt a lot better. I was on my way to having friends!

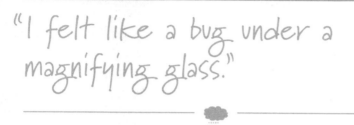

"I felt like a bug under a magnifying glass."

Still Invisible

But the next morning was a repeat of the day before. The same kids ran up to each other, but no one talked to me. I drifted from one place to the next, feeling invisible. Then, in class, someone finally talked to me.

"What's your shoe size?" one boy asked. Another kid said, "Yeah! How much do you eat?" A girl chimed in with, "How tall are you?" Instead of asking my name, everyone was focusing on my size! I *am* small, but at my old school, no one seemed to care. Now I felt like a bug being examined under a magnifying glass. Maybe they weren't trying to be mean, but it hurt.

The Tears Come

Finally, I couldn't take it anymore. I ran out of the classroom as tears ran down my cheeks. I had gotten what I wanted—I had been noticed—but no one saw the *real* me!

After that, no one invited me to sit with them at lunch. I tried to look busy when people walked by, but sitting alone every day hurt. I dreaded lunch—and everything else about school.

The weeks became months, and I wasn't even close to having friends. Sometimes kids made rude comments about my height, and I started to feel so shy and self-conscious that I wouldn't start up a conversation with *anyone*. I began to think that I was *meant* to be alone!

"Lunch Friends"

Then one day I was running the mile for track when I accidentally shouldered a girl named Lauren. I thought she might get mad, but she just said it was okay. A few days later, Lauren started running with me! Before long, I started sitting with Lauren and her friends at lunch.

I didn't talk much at first. What if I said the wrong thing? It was such a relief to have friends—even just eat-lunch-together friends—that I didn't want to risk it. But as I sat there day after day, I finally stopped worrying and started to just be myself.

"Finally I stopped worrying and started to just be myself."

The Stories Were Wrong

That's when I realized something. All those stories about "the new girl" were just wrong. You can't always walk into a new place and become a part of the group overnight. Sometimes, it takes time. Because I'd had a bad experience in the beginning, I'd just given up on making friends. I should have hung in there and kept trying, because if you do, you *will* find friends. *Really.*

ONE DAY, A FEW WEEKS AFTER I STARTED SITTING WITH them at lunch, Lauren and a few girls were talking about going to the mall after school. "Would you like to go with us?" they asked.

"Mom!" I yelled when I got home. *"I got invited to the mall!"* It was one of the best days of my life.

DG Poll

44%

of girls have been the new kid at school.

Chapter Three

WHEN PARENTS LET YOU DOWN

I'm So Disappointed in My Dad

By Diane,* age 12, Nev.

*I*F YOU MET MY DAD, YOU'D PROBABLY think he was a great guy. He's so fun and charming. When I was little, I loved him a lot. I guess that's why it was so hard to face up to the fact that he is just a big phony.

My dad has a drinking problem and he lies, even to the people he supposedly loves. When he drinks, he gets really mean. He and my mom used to have terrible fights, and sometimes he would hit her. When I was little, I didn't really understand how bad my dad was. My grandma—my dad's mom—used to tell me that it was my mom's fault that my dad acted the way he did, and I believed her.

When I was eight, my mom decided to leave my dad. She was afraid of what he might do, so she went to court and got a restraining order against him. That meant that he had to stay away from us, and if he didn't, he could be put in jail.

"My dad had to stay away from us, or he could be put in jail."

Arrested

My mom and I had gone to stay with my grandma, just until we could get a place of our own. One night my dad got drunk and then showed up at my grandma's house, yelling for my mom. When my dad started throwing things and threatening my mom, my mom and I ran to the neighbors' house for help. Finally the police arrived and arrested my dad.

A Trial—Then Jail

Because my dad had broken the restraining order, there was a trial, and my mom sent me to stay with my other grandparents—my mom's parents—in another state. I was gone for six weeks, and when I came back, my dad was in jail, serving a two-year sentence.

During those two years I got a few letters from my dad. He told me he was sorry, that he'd never act like that again, and that he couldn't wait to see me. I wanted so badly for it all to be true that I believed he'd changed. I was sure he'd be the dad I wanted him to be.

"I still love my dad but I know now that I can't trust him."

Let Down Again

After he was released, we set up a time to meet at a restaurant. I was nervous, but I was excited, too. I thought things would be different now...but he didn't even show up! I kept making excuses for him, like he didn't know exactly where we were supposed to meet. I guess I should have realized then that he'd never change, but it still didn't sink in.

For the next year my dad said he was traveling around, and then he settled down a long way from where I live. He had a new girlfriend who seemed really nice, so when she said he wasn't drinking, I was ready to visit them and give him another chance.

At first the visit went okay, but then my dad and his girlfriend got into an argument, and he hit her. I was so scared! Nothing had changed—he was still the same!

"I don't know if I'll ever be able to completely let go of all the hurt and anger."

Not that Kind of Dad

I've finally realized that no matter how sincere my dad seems when he tells me he's sorry and that everything is going to be different, I can't believe him. He's just not going to become the kind of dad I always wanted him to be.

I've been through so much hurt and anger because of my dad. There were times when I felt like there must be something I could do to make him change, and when nothing I did made a difference, I got very depressed. To make things worse, I felt like I couldn't even talk to my friends about it. No one else had family problems like mine. How could they understand?

Getting Help

I'm lucky, though, because my mom made sure I got counseling. My mom and I have learned that it's important to talk about everything. I've been in group counseling with three other girls, all with family problems. Hearing about their experiences—some a lot worse than mine—made me realize that I wasn't the only one who'd been through something like this.

One thing I've realized from all this is that I don't like people to feel sorry for me for what has happened. I also learned that my dad has the problem, not me, and that the things I've been through don't give me an excuse to say or do mean things, no matter how angry or hurt I feel inside.

A New Start

Things have gotten much better for my mom and me. She remarried, so now I have a great stepdad. Instead of thinking about how much my dad has hurt me, I try to focus on the good things in my life. I don't know if I'll ever be able to completely let go of all my anger, but it's getting easier.

IF YOU'RE GOING THROUGH SOMETHING LIKE THIS, remember that you aren't alone and that it's not your fault. You don't have to keep it a secret! When I finally told other people about my dad, I found out that other kids had gone through similar things. Talking things out helped me a lot, and it will help you, too.

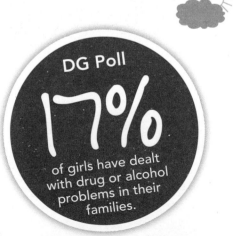

DG Poll

17%

of girls have dealt with drug or alcohol problems in their families.

"My stepdad never came right out and told me that he wanted to end our visits..."

My Stepdad Doesn't Love Me

By Megan,* age 12, Ontario

*All names have been changed.

MY MEMORIES HAVE BEEN

scarred for life, thanks to the man I used to call "Dad." He was actually my stepdad, but I never really thought of him as a "step"—from as far back I could remember, he was always just "Dad" or "Daddy." He was a great dad, too. He'd cheer me on from the sidelines at soccer games, take me to dance lessons and swimming practice, and even help out in my classroom at school. When I was little, I *knew* I could count on him to be there forever.

My mom and stepdad divorced when I was seven. They'd been separated for a few years, so I was used to him not living with us. I didn't think the divorce would change anything. And it didn't, at first. My stepdad still picked me up every Wednesday night so we could go visit his parents—my Nanny and Grandpa—and we still spent every Sunday together. When he dropped me off on Sunday nights, he'd tell me that he loved me—that he'd *always* love me. Nothing could change that...or so I thought.

> "I knew I could count on my stepdad to be there forever."

Cancelled Plans

But things *did* start to change. My stepdad had a girlfriend, Stephanie. I really liked her, and I thought she liked me, too. But as things got more serious between them, Stephanie stopped being so nice. She didn't want my stepdad to take me places on Sundays anymore, and he started cancelling our plans. There were even times when he just didn't show up when he was supposed to.

How Do I Get Him Back?

My stepdad never came right out and told me that he wanted to end our visits—he just gradually pulled away. He never explained why, either. I thought he was mad at me. I wanted to ask, but I was afraid he'd get even madder. Instead, I just tried really hard to be good so that he would still love me.

"I felt like my dad didn't love me anymore."

No Stepdaughters Allowed

When I first found out my stepdad and Stephanie were getting married, I kept asking if I could go to the wedding. My stepdad would say things like, "I don't know when it will be," which really confused me. How could he not know when his own wedding was? Eventually I figured out that they just didn't want me there.

Once they were married, my dad and Stephanie wanted me around even less. When they had a baby, I asked to see her. The answer was no. They wouldn't even give me a picture for my scrapbook.

Time to Give Up

My stepdad had been paying child support for me, but he wanted to stop paying, so he and my mom ended up in court.

My mom said we could also fight for my right to continue seeing him more often. In some ways I wanted to, but after thinking long and hard about it, I decided not to. I didn't know how to make him love me like a daughter again, no matter how badly I wanted it. Once I'd made that decision, our relationship was over for good.

I'd like to say I've gotten over the hurt, but it's not really true. I think I'll always carry some of it with me, but at least I understand some things better now. For one thing, I know that what happened wasn't my fault. My stepdad pushed me out of his life because *he* wasn't strong enough to deal with a complicated family, not because I wasn't good enough.

Lucky...and Strong

I also know that I'm really lucky. I have a great mom, and I *know* I'm strong. For a few years now, I've been involved in synchronized swimming, and I'm one of the top swimmers on a nationally competing team. All that hard work has helped to give me self-confidence and taught me to believe in myself.

SOMETIMES I FEEL SAD WHEN I SEE OTHER GIRLS' DADS cheering them on. But then I think, *That's his loss.* My stepdad didn't turn out to be the kind of person I needed him to be, but I'm not going to let that stop me from being the best person *I* can be.

DG Poll

13%

of girls have had trouble with a stepmom, stepdad, or step siblings.

Chapter Four

TOUGH TIMES FOR FAMILIES

My Dad Lost His Job

By Janine, age 12, Calif.

M

Y FAMILY HAS MOVED A LOT, SO I've gotten pretty used to walking into a new school and making new friends. It doesn't even bother me that much—I always know I'll feel at home in the new place after a few months. But about a year ago we moved again, and that time it was completely different. We'd only been in our latest home for eight months, so when my parents told my brothers and me that we were moving yet again, I was really surprised. But the reason we were moving was the biggest shock of all: My father had lost his job.

> "Suddenly the security I'd totally taken for granted was just gone."

And that wasn't even the worst of it. My father had been fired because he had cancer. So now he had a terrible illness and no job. In fact, neither of my parents could work for a while, since my mom had to give up her job in order to be with my dad while he got the treatment he needed to get well. I couldn't imagine how we would manage—what if neither of my parents could find work again? Suddenly the security I'd totally taken for granted was just gone. It was scary.

Turned Upside-Down

While my parents went to another city for my dad's medical care and to look for work, my younger brothers and I moved into my grandparents' apartment. Between starting at a new school in the middle of the year, being away from our parents, and worrying about the future, our lives were turned completely upside down. My youngest brother, who was only four at the time, was too young to really understand what was happening. But I took it very hard, and so did my 10-year-old brother, Luke.

Changes in My Brother

Luke and I have always been close, but after my parents left he shut out everyone, even me. I missed my parents so much, and not being able to feel close to my brother made it even worse. And on top of everything else, I was worried about him. He had started to develop facial "tics"—jerky little twitches of the muscles in his face. Even though I understood that they were caused by all the fear and anger he was feeling, the change in him scared me even more.

"I cried a lot, and for the first time in my life, I started to hate school."

No One Would Understand

I wanted to keep my faith in my parents, I really did. I knew they were counting on us, and I didn't want to disappoint them. But I was so sad and angry that for a long time, I just did the easiest thing: I gave in to all those crushing feelings. I cried a lot, and for the first time in my life, I started to hate school. I didn't even try to make friends. *Why bother?* I thought. We'd just be leaving again soon, and they'd never become *real* friends, anyway. How could anyone possibly understand what I was going through? I kept to myself so much in the first month that most people decided I was selfish and unfriendly.

Friends for Hard Times

Luckily, there were two girls at my school who reached out to me. They asked me questions about my life. Why had I moved to Florida? Why was I living with my grandparents? Where were my parents? When I finally started to talk, it was such a relief to share all the pain and fear I'd been holding inside. And Melissa and Nicole really listened. They seemed to understand what I was going through, even though I'd been convinced no one would. Their caring warmed me up so much that pretty soon I had a whole group of friends. I still wanted my family back to normal, but I stopped hating school, and my problems became much easier to bear.

"I met the best friends I'll ever have. They'll always be in my heart."

I'm happy to say that life is back to normal now. It wasn't easy and it didn't go by fast, but my dad did get better, and my parents eventually found work and a new home for us. The day we all moved back in together was one of the happiest days of my life. A few months later, Luke's tics gradually disappeared, too, and our relationship returned to normal.

True Best Friends

All of which goes to show you that when one door closes forever, at the other end of the hallway a window opens, allowing the sunshine to make its way back in. I was so wrong to think that I wouldn't make close, lasting friendships during those hard times. I met the best friends I'll ever have, and I know now that they'll always be in my heart.

I ALSO LEARNED SOMETHING REALLY IMPORTANT DURING those hard times: You don't have to go through the bad times alone. If you shut yourself off, it just makes everything more painful. When all you want to do is crawl into a dark hole and be left alone, reaching out may seem like the hardest thing to do—but it's also the very best way to help yourself. I know that now, and the next time trouble comes around, I won't forget it.

DG Poll

18%

of girls have been stressed by their parent losing his or her job.

Drugs Changed My Cousin's Life Forever

By Ashlee, age 12, Texas

"I felt like I was in a horrible nightmare. Mike was my cousin, not a drug addict!"

M

Y COUSIN MIKE* AND I HAVE always been very close. Our families are close, too, so we've grown up spending a lot of time together. Even though he's six years older than I am, we've always had a special connection. Mike is like the older brother I never had, but even better, because we've never had to share a house or parents!

When Mike was 16 and I was 10, things started to change. It seemed like he was distancing himself from everyone in our family, including me. He'd started high school and was working at a grocery store, too, so it didn't seem *that* surprising that we didn't see him as often as before. But what was surprising was the way he acted. When I saw him on the street, he was cold. He'd glare at me, or just ignore me. Sometimes it felt like he was just being mean for no reason. One time I asked him if he wanted to play basketball. "Leave me alone, Ashlee," was all he said. I thought maybe he was just having a bad day, so I tried to let it go. When I saw him a couple of days later, I smiled at him, but all I got in return was that *glare*. It broke my heart, but I did my best to shrug it off.

"Mike's glare broke my heart, but I did my best to shrug it off."

What's Going On?
Then one night my dad suddenly rushed out of the house and was gone for a long time. I couldn't figure out what was going

*Name has been changed.

on, but finally my parents sat me down and explained everything. My aunt had just found out that Mike was on drugs, and had been for over a year. I felt like I was in a horrible nightmare. Mike was my cousin, not a drug addict! I was shocked. I cried for hours and hours.

Confused and Miserable

It was hard to go on as if everything was okay, but I knew that I had to. So I went to school and did my homework and everything else I usually do, even though I had so many feelings crashing around inside me that I felt confused and miserable most of the time.

"I started to think I hated Mike, and I'd never be able to forgive him."

Sometimes all I could think about was how worried I was. At the time, my class had been learning about how drugs can really hurt your body, and I was scared that whatever Mike was taking would kill him. But mostly, I was angry. I had looked up to Mike and believed in him, and now, suddenly, I couldn't anymore. And to make it even worse, he didn't want to get help—not at first, anyway. I couldn't understand how he could hurt his family—*my* family—like that, not to mention himself. I started to think I hated him, and that I'd never be able to forgive him. But I also felt like I should still love him, and forgive him, too.

Luckily, I was able to talk to my mom and dad about what was going on inside me. My dad helped me realize that I did still love Mike, and that the reason I was so worried was precisely *because* I loved him so much. And my mom helped me realize that loving someone includes forgiving them, even when they do something terrible.

I Had My Cousin Back!

I didn't see Mike for a long time. First he went away to a drug treatment home for troubled teens, and then he went to live with his dad. Finally he started coming to his mom's house on the weekends. He seemed happier and more relaxed than he had before. Then, after Christmas break, he came back home. One night, we all played Scrabble, and he was laughing and enjoying himself, like he used to. I finally started to feel like I had my cousin back.

"The drugs tore my family apart, but that tear has been sewn back up."

Getting Better

It's summer now, and Mike and I are spending a lot of time together again. We have a great time, and it makes me really happy. I know this has been a long, hard road for him, and it's not over yet. He's still in therapy with a doctor, and he's working again, and going to summer school so he can graduate. I'm sure that's not easy, but I'm also sure he knows now how much I love him (as does the rest of my family) and that we will always be here for him.

I KNOW MIKE HAS LEARNED A LOT FROM THIS EXPERIENCE, and he's not the only one. I have, too. I've learned how important it is to stand by the people you love when they're in trouble. The drugs tore my family apart, but that tear has been sewn back up, thanks to a lot of love and time spent together. I've also learned not to judge someone on one mistake, or one part of their lives. I realized that the problems Mike had were just one small part of who is, not the whole picture. In spite of his addiction, I think he's one of the greatest people I know.

If you learn one thing from my story, I hope it will be to love and support the people you care about, all the time—even when they make mistakes.

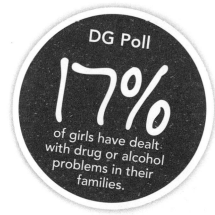

DG Poll

17%

of girls have dealt with drug or alcohol problems in their families.

Robbed at Gunpoint

By Morgan, age 11, Fla.

*T*HE DAY STARTED LIKE MOST SATURDAYS. My mom and I ate breakfast and then drove to my rehearsal. I'd been lucky enough to be chosen to be in the chorus of the opera *Hansel and Gretel* at a local theater. It was just a small part, but the chance to work with professionals was a dream come true. When we arrived at the center, we couldn't find a parking space, so we parked on a side street around the corner. Then I opened the door to get out.

Suddenly there was a man in front of me, blocking my way and leaning into the car. He was filthy, and he smelled terrible. He put his hand on my leg, pinning me to the seat, and pointed a gun at my mom. I screamed—I've never been so scared in my life! I was so terrified I almost felt like I was watching the whole scene—like it was happening to someone else. I was too shocked to even think, but my mom reacted quickly. She threw her purse at him, and he grabbed it and took off on his bike.

"The thief hadn't just stolen my mom's purse, he'd also taken my sense of well-being."

I Thought I Was Fine

We just sat there, shaking, and then my mom used her cell phone to call 911. I felt better—safer—after the police officer got there, but even so, I didn't want to get out of the car at first. But by the time we'd answered all of his questions, I was feeling a lot calmer, so I decided to go to the rehearsal in spite of what had happened. I thought I was fine.

But the next day, I wasn't fine—not at all. I was afraid to get in a car, especially my mom's car. The fear was so bad, I didn't want to go anywhere, not to school or even to rehearsal, which I loved. When I *had* to go somewhere, I was a wreck. I'd get really nervous whenever the car stopped, even if was just for a red light. Even though I knew better, I couldn't stop thinking that someone would try to get into the car the minute it stopped moving. The thief hadn't just stolen my mom's purse, he'd also taken something from me—something much more valuable than money or credit cards. He'd stolen my sense of well-being.

> "I was living with so much fear that I just couldn't be rational. My emotions were in control."

My Parents Didn't Understand

My parents tried to help. They kept saying, "It's okay. No one got hurt. It's over." They couldn't understand that I really *did* get hurt. I just didn't have any scratches or bruises or broken bones, because all my wounds were on the inside.

As time went by, things got worse instead of better. I started to be afraid of anyone with dark skin or dreadlocks—anyone who looked at all like that guy. In my head I knew that wasn't fair, but I couldn't help it. I was living with so much fear that I just couldn't be rational about it. My emotions were in control, not my mind.

Finally my parents found a counselor for me to talk to. I told her how scared I was, and even that I'd been really mad at my mom. She hadn't fought back at all—she'd just given the guy her purse! But after talking to the counselor I realized that my mom actually *had* done the right thing. If she hadn't given the guy what he wanted, we might have gotten hurt.

"I know now that I am a strong person and a survivor."

My Power
The counselor also helped me realize that I was letting this man have too much control over my life. She told me that I could take that power away from him if I wanted to. Maybe we couldn't get my mom's purse back, but I could steal *me* back from him.

The counselor showed me that the only way to overcome my fears was to face them—and that meant doing the things that scared me most. It was hard, buy my parents helped by insisting that I confront difficult situations, and by going through them with me. I also got so tired of missing out on things I really wanted to do that I just refused to let my fear stop me anymore.

Not Living in Fear
It's been over a year now, and things are much better. I still get scared sometimes, and I still find myself misjudging someone

just because he looks like the man who robbed us. But now I recognize what's happening, and I deal with it. I don't live in fear anymore.

I BELIEVE THAT THINGS HAPPEN FOR A REASON. I LEARNED A LOT FROM this. For one thing, I'm much more aware of my surroundings than I used to be, and that's a good thing. But even better, I learned a lot about myself. I know now that I am a strong person and a survivor. And I'm sure of one thing: I won't ever let anyone take me away from me again.

DG Poll

34%

of girls have been seriously worried about their safety at home or at school.

Chapter Five

LOSS

My Broken Family

By Torrie, age 13, Ariz.

Y

OU HAVE A MOTHER AND FATHER who are madly in love (you think), a huge house, a kind, loving family, wonderful vacations, and just about anything you could ever ask for.

Then—*poof!* It all goes up in smoke. Suddenly, your parents are divorced, you've moved into a much smaller house, and you're not getting much of anything you want anymore. What do you do with all the anger and hurt? How do you keep your life from spinning out of control?

"My parents had been fighting a lot, but I thought they would work it out."

The Downward Spiral

I used to be a straight-A student. I got along with my parents, my teachers, other kids—everyone, really. I *did* like to eat, and sometimes, I'd eat just because I felt like eating, not because I was hungry. I was a little bit overweight, but only a little. It wasn't a huge problem.

And then my parents split up. I'll never forget the day my mom told me. The first thing she said was, "It's not your fault." *What?* I thought. *What's not my fault?*

"Your father and I have decided to get a divorce," she went on. I was stunned. I knew my parents had been fighting a lot, but I thought it was just something they were going through. I thought they'd work it out. But a divorce?

Everything Changed

Right away, everything changed. We stopped doing things as a family. If my parents had to be at some event together, they avoided each other like poison. I'd watch them from across the room, willing them to talk to each other. I kept thinking, *If I can somehow do or say the right thing, we'll be a real family again.*

It didn't happen. My dad moved out of the house, and then my mom and I had to move, too. I hated my new neighborhood, and I hated hearing that there was no money for the things I'd always taken for granted.

"My grades slid to C's, and I started getting into trouble."

My anger grew. My grades slid to C's, and I started getting into trouble. I was rude to people, even people I knew cared about me. I knew it was wrong, but spreading my misery around was one way to let it out. It made me feel better, at least for a little while.

Overweight

Eating made me feel better, too. The angrier I got, the more I ate. Instead of being a little heavy, I became seriously overweight. Kids at school began to pick on me. I'd come home and stare into the mirror, crying and thinking I looked hideous.

The Picture in My Mind

Then came my bat mitzvah. My parents had been separated for some time by then. Still, I'd imagined that that day would be different somehow. In my mind, I'd always pictured my parents standing side by side, beaming at me, proud of what I had accomplished.

"The angrier I got, the more I ate."

It didn't happen like that. My parents stayed as far away from each other as possible. I was so disappointed I felt like crying. But the way they acted made me realize something. If my parents couldn't get together for something as important as my bat mitzvah, they'd never be able to. They'd chosen to be apart, and there was nothing I could do to change that.

You might think that realization would have made me feel worse, and in a way, it did. But it also set me free. I realized that, although I couldn't change their lives, I could change mine. I could accept this new life and find a way to make the best of it. To do that, I had to find more positive ways of releasing my pain. The only question was, *how*?

Finding an Answer

For me, the answer was to control my eating and start exercising. If I liked the way I looked, I'd feel better about myself and my life, too. The first weight-loss program I tried was a disaster, but then I found one that worked for me. I signed up for a synchronized swimming class and dance lessons. They gave me a way to work off some of my anger, and they also took my mind off the negative things happening at home. I began to feel cheery and full of life when I was swimming—as if anything was possible!

I dropped 20 pounds. I got along better with my teachers, and my grades improved. As I began to feel better about myself, I stopped caring so much when kids teased me. I had friends, *real* friends who had stood by me when things were really bad.

Still Torn in Two

I still have to live with the changes my parents' divorce brought to my life. The holidays are especially tough for me. At a time when families are supposed to be so close, I end up torn in two directions. Some days, I think my parents were selfish to divorce. I feel like they should have stayed together for me, even if their marriage wasn't perfect.

BUT MOSTLY, I'VE GOTTEN MORE COMFORTABLE WITH THE situation. I can even see that some good things came from the divorce. For one thing, I don't have to listen to my parents fighting anymore! But more important, I found a strength inside myself I never knew I had. I can't change the fact that my parents are divorced, but I *can* change my reaction to it. And that's made all the difference.

DG Poll

13%

of girls have been stressed by their parents' divorce.

My Mom Died

By Mackenzie, age 13, Ore.

I KNEW SOMETHING WAS WRONG.

My little brother and I were eating dinner when we heard our parents whispering in the other room. We went into the kitchen and saw that our parents were crying. I asked what was wrong, and my mom said that she had cancer again.

When I was four, my mom had been sick, but she'd had treatment and the cancer went away. We all thought that was the end of it. Since I was really young at the time, I didn't really know what cancer was anyway. All I knew was that my mom had gotten better, and that was all that mattered.

"I mean, nothing bad could happen to my mom, right?"

But even six years later, I still didn't really know what cancer meant for my mom. I mean, nothing bad could happen to my mom, right? My friend's mom and one of my mom's friends were also diagnosed with cancer, so it seemed like lots of people were going through the same thing. *Maybe it isn't really that bad,* I thought. *Maybe it's normal, even.*

Waiting for a Cure

My mom and her friends all went through chemotherapy—a treatment for cancer. The chemotherapy drugs help kill the cancer, but they can also make all your hair fall out, so for months my mom and her friends wore wigs, scarves, and hats. Eventually all her hair started growing back, and the cancer seemed to be backing off. My friend's mom was cured—just like that. I was happy for my friend, but I was also secretly jealous. I wanted my mom to get better, too.

As I got older, I began to realize how serious my mom's illness was. My parents were traveling all over the country—and even to Mexico—to find a cure, and it was getting harder for my mom to walk. When she did, she limped. It wasn't long before she was in bed all the time, too weak to get up.

"I began to realize how serious my mom's illness was."

So Weak

One day I came home from school and couldn't find anybody. I finally found my brother, who said that our mom was in the hospital. When my dad came home, he took us there. I was happy to be going to see my mom, but that changed when I actually saw her. She could barely breathe or drink on her own—it just took too much effort. It really hurt to see her like that.

After about a week in the hospital, my mom came home. I was so happy because I thought that meant she was better. But she wasn't. Then one night as I said goodnight and hugged her, she said, "I'm going to try to live to be around with you, but if I'm not, just know that you are going to do fine in life." I told her that of course she was going to be around for me, and that I loved her too much for her to not be there!

Time to Say Goodbye

The next day I went to school with butterflies in my stomach. I knew my mom had gotten worse overnight. During second period, the principal came to get me. It was time for me to go home and say goodbye.

"I started to cry hard and took my mom's hand. I told her I loved her."

My mom wasn't talking right and her eyes were rolled back into her head. I started to cry very hard and took her hand. I heard her say my name and that she loved me. I told her I loved her too. She made a weird sound, and I knew that she was gone. I cried and cried.

I didn't go to school for the rest of the week. At her memorial service, people talked about how loving my mom was. On the piano, I played two songs by Enya, my mom's favorite composer. Playing for my mom and hearing everyone say such nice things about her made me feel so good that for a while, I forgot to be sad.

Life Without Mom

The day my mom died, I closed my eyes and tried to picture my life without her. I couldn't. In a month, I would turn 13—I'd be a teenager—and I needed my mom for that! But as a little time has passed, I realized that when I just *think* about her, I feel confident and strong. I recently went skiing for the first time, and as I started going down a really steep hill, I was frightened. Then, all of a sudden, I wasn't scared anymore. I couldn't help thinking my mom had something to do with that. I think my mom is now my guardian angel, always watching over me and giving me the strength to be brave and happy—the way she wants me to be.

WHENEVER I *DO* FEEL BAD, I LIKE TO THINK ABOUT THE time my mom and I went snorkeling in Hawaii. As the clear water swirled around us, I saw some big fish and sharp coral. I was scared, but my mom took my hand and said that the big fish weren't going to hurt me. Since she was brave enough to go underwater, I knew I was, too. Everything was blue, yellow, and orange, and the sun streamed through the water in beams. Life was all around us. It was just the fish, my mom, and me. I felt really close to her, and safe. I just wanted to stay there, with my mom, forever.

DG Poll

54%

of girls say someone they love has died.

Chapter Six

MAKING AMENDS

Can't We Just Rewind?

By Kristy, age 13, Calif.

I'VE ALWAYS CONSIDERED MYSELF SUPER-LUCKY to part of a really tight group. Last year, there were about 10 of us in all, both boys and girls, and we were as close as friends can get. The last thing I expected was for it all to fall apart.

I was slogging my way through my math homework one night when the phone rang. It was my friends Zack and Jeremy—guys in our group—calling to talk. After a few minutes, they started asking me questions about our other friends. "Who do you like the most?" and "Who do you like the least?" Then the questions got tougher: "What do you think of Taylor?" "Did you ever notice how much Courtney talks about her grades?" "Does Brandon ever annoy you?"

"Jeremy was playing our conversation back for everyone."

A Big Mistake

Without giving it much thought, I answered: I liked Alexis best; I didn't really like Eric; sometimes Taylor acted stuck up; Courtney *did* brag about her grades a *lot*; I hated Brandon's dumb jokes. And it went on. Jeremy and Zack seemed to be hanging on every word, and it was impossible to resist all that attention. The words just flew out my mouth.

During second period the next day, Jeremy started passing around a tape recorder. Soon all my friends were whispering behind their hands and glaring at me. I asked my friend Courtney what was up, but she just turned her back on me. Finally Alexis clued me in: Jeremy and Zack had recorded our conversation the night before, and Jeremy was playing it back for everyone. By the end of class, all my friends hated me.

What Do I Do Now?

I thought back to the conversation the night before, remembering everything I'd said, and I started to feel sick. I had just been talking, blowing off steam! I never meant for any of those things to be repeated! There was no getting around it, though: I'd said some really mean things. My whole world seemed to be crashing down on me. What was I supposed to do now?! Just like that, I'd lost my friends—every one of them!

"By the end of class, all my friends hated me."

I faked a stomachache and spilled the whole story to my mom in the car. When we got home, she called the school and told one of the counselors. The counselor promptly took away Jeremy's tape recorder. He and Zack were both sent home for the day. Although I hadn't asked my mom to call the school, I felt a little better when I heard that. But in a way, it didn't matter at all, because it was too late to undo what they'd done—and what *I'd* done.

Saying Sorry

The last thing I wanted was to go to school the next day and face everyone. But I wanted my friends back, and I figured that the only chance I had to make things right was to apologize. So the next day, I found everyone I'd hurt and told them how important they were to me, and how sorry I was for what I'd said. And I *was* sorry. Jeremy and Zack were dead wrong to record our conversation, but I had been careless, and I felt terrible.

"My best friends understood I had not wanted to cause anyone pain."

Better but Still Different

It took weeks for things to return to normal. Our group still ate lunch together every day, but the atmosphere was definitely strained. Some of my friends were afraid to talk to me because they thought it would look like they were taking sides. Some, including Alexis, stuck by me. I had a hard time forgiving myself for hurting people I cared about, but my closest friends understood that I had not wanted to cause anyone pain.

I never did find out why Jeremy and Zack recorded our conversation. At one point Zack told me that they'd called another girl first, but she wasn't home—so it wasn't even like they were out to get me. In the end, though, it didn't really matter why they did it. All I really cared about was regaining the trust of the friends I'd let down.

The Big Picture

I've learned a lot from this experience. I learned that even when you feel like your whole world is falling apart, things aren't as bad as they seem. I cried and stressed out so much that horrible day, but it really wasn't the end of the world. And I learned that I had friends who would stick by me no matter what—even when I felt like I might not deserve their support.

MOST IMPORTANT, I LEARNED THAT WORDS YOU TOSS OFF casually can come back to bite you. If you take away anything from this story, I hope it's that you should *never* talk about your friends behind their backs, even to other friends. The next time you find yourself getting drawn into one of *those* conversations, stop and ask yourself if what you're saying would pass the "tape recorder test." If it wouldn't...zip it. I sure wish I had!

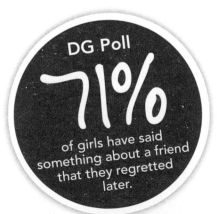

DG Poll

71%

of girls have said something about a friend that they regretted later.

"The person that I had tried so hard to get to like me all of a sudden hated my guts."

I Toilet-Papered My Teacher's House

By Camille, age 12, La.

I HAD SOME GREAT TEACHERS IN SIXTH grade, but I loved Mrs. Anderson* the most. She was young, pretty, funny, and she seemed to really like kids. We learned a lot in her class, but it was fun too—you just had to keep listening to see what she'd say next.

I admired Mrs. Anderson so much, I was almost obsessed with her. I wanted her to think I was special, just like I thought she was special. I e-mailed her a few times, telling her how great I thought she was—and she answered me, too. I know teachers aren't supposed to have favorite students, but deep inside I was pretty sure I was one of hers.

"I admired Mrs. Anderson so much, I was almost obsessed with her."

Rolling for Fun

The girls in my town are big on "rolling"— covering someone's yard and trees with toilet paper. We do it to people we like. The year before we'd rolled Mrs. Gruber, our fifth-grade teacher, and she'd thought it was funny. So one Friday night, my friends Cammie and Madeline and I decided that it would be fun to roll Mrs. Anderson, too. It never even occurred to us that we might make our teacher mad—not funny, easygoing Mrs. Anderson!

All of the adults' names in this story have been changed.

My mom drove us to Mrs. Anderson's house, and we quickly draped trees, bushes, and the lawn with long strips of toilet paper. The porch light came on and we ran for the car, laughing and feeling on top of the world.

"I wanted to crawl in a box and never come out."

Back at Madeline's house, we left a message on Mrs. Anderson's voicemail, saying we'd rolled her. Then we called most of the kids in our class, too. Not realizing we'd already called her to "confess," a couple of the boys we'd talked to also called Mrs. Anderson's house—twice. The second time, Mr. Anderson answered, and he was not happy. He told the boys not to call there again, *ever*.

Rolling...in Trouble?

A few minutes later, the phone rang at Madeline's house. It was Mrs. Anderson, and she was *furious*. We'd gone way too far, she said, and she was upset that the boys kept calling. She was so mad she'd even called our principal, Dr. Breyer!

I felt like the entire world had ended. I wanted to crawl in a box and never come out. The person that I had tried so hard to get to like me all of a sudden hated my guts. How could something we'd done for fun turn out so wrong?

Mom Intervenes

I called my mom in tears. She felt terrible, too, since she was the one who'd driven us there. She called Mrs. Anderson to explain that we'd only wanted to show her how much we loved her. Mrs. Anderson said that she understood that, but that we needed to understand that she and her husband wanted to keep their work lives and personal lives separate. She felt it was inappropriate for her students to have her phone number and address.

> "I knew Mrs. Anderson would hold a grudge against me forever."

Too Worried to Eat

I cried all weekend, and my stomach was so tied up in knots that I couldn't eat. My parents tried to convince me that it would all blow over soon enough, but I knew I'd ruined everything. Mrs. Anderson would hold a grudge against me forever.

At school on Monday, we had an assembly about the rolling. Our names weren't mentioned, but the teachers explained that rolling was considered vandalism and could be a felony—a serious crime you can go to jail for! Cammie, Madeline, and I stared at the floor the whole time, too ashamed to look anyone in the eye. The teachers made it sound like we'd been *trying* to do something hurtful. I felt like no one understood, least of all Mrs. Anderson, the one person I cared most about.

Apologizing

I was so scared to face Mrs. Anderson again, but I also really wanted her to know how sorry I was. So after school, Cammie, Madeline, and I went to talk to her. Mrs. Anderson said she accepted our apology, but I thought she still seemed mad. I walked out of her classroom feeling heartbroken, still sure I was on her "bad" list forever.

I was wrong, though. Mrs. Anderson really *did* accept my apology, because after that day, she went right back to treating me the way she always had—like a student she really liked and cared about. I felt awkward around her at first, but as time went by, I started to believe that things really were okay between us.

SO IT TURNED OUT MY PARENTS WERE RIGHT: LIFE *DOES* GO on. I realize now that not everyone sees things the way I do, and I've learned to think a little harder before I act. But most of all, I've learned that even if you make a *huge* mistake, people can forgive you, especially if you mean well and do your best to apologize. I sure don't plan to get in trouble again any time soon—and I definitely won't be rolling any more houses—but it *is* nice to find out that messing up isn't the end of the world.

DG Poll

39%

of girls have gotten in serious trouble at home or at school.

Chapter Seven

LIVING WITH DISABILITIES

I Am Not Stupid!

By Samantha, age 8, Calif.

H

AVE YOU EVER REALLY, REALLY wanted to do something, but no matter how hard you tried, you just couldn't seem to get the hang of it? That's what learning to read was like for me.

When I was in kindergarten I loved books, so I couldn't wait to learn to read. I thought it would be so great to read my books all by myself. I didn't have trouble at first, when we were just learning our letters—I was one of the best in my class. But by first grade everyone caught up to me, and then they all passed me. They were all sounding out words, but I couldn't do it. Even though I tried hard, I just didn't get it.

> "I felt stupid, and I worried that maybe I'd never learn to read."

I Thought I Was Reading

Still, it wasn't too bad in first grade, because I wasn't the only one—other kids had trouble reading, too. Also, the books were pretty simple, and I have a great memory, so I could get by. I could remember a story so well I could "read" it if I had to. I even thought I *was* reading it, but I wasn't—I was just saying it from memory.

Then I got to second grade, and it got a lot harder. I still wasn't even reading at a kindergarten level. One day the teacher passed out copies of a book no one had ever seen before. Most of the other kids could read it, but I couldn't. Some of them were doing so well they were reading books like Harry Potter, but I was still stuck on Dr. Seuss. They'd say things like, "I can read that whole book in a minute, and you can't even read the first paragraph that fast." I felt stupid, and I worried that maybe I'd never learn to read.

"My parents thought I just wasn't trying hard enough, even though I was!"

Am I Stupid?

I was really frustrated, and so were my teacher and my mom. They thought I just wasn't trying hard enough, even though I was! My mom would sit with me while I did my homework, trying to help me with my spelling words and reading. Sometimes she would yell at me, or tell me I just needed to concentrate more, but it didn't help.

No matter how hard I tried, I just couldn't get it. If I tried to sound out a word, I'd start off okay, and get the first couple of letters, but then I'd just make up the rest of the word. I'd look at a word like "good," and I'd get the "g" and the "o," but I'd think the word was "gosh," not "good." Sometimes, during silent reading time in school, I'd read a whole story like that. When I got to the end, it was as if I'd read a totally different story than everyone else!

Dumber than Ever

The worst part was reading aloud in class. It was so embarrassing not being able to do something that most kids thought was easy. I'd take longer than everyone else, and I'd get all the words wrong. It was so bad that after a while the teacher stopped calling on me to read. In one way, that was a relief—but I also felt left out, and dumber than ever.

I was lucky, though, because even before I finished second grade, my mom and dad realized that something was wrong. They took me to a place called Lindamood-Bell, which has teachers who are trained to help kids like me. I had to take a bunch of tests, and afterward, they told my parents that I needed tutoring—classes with just me and a teacher—to help me catch up.

"It was embarrassing not being able to do something most kids thought was easy."

Finally—Everything Clicked

I was scared to go to tutoring at first. I didn't want to leave my school and my friends. I didn't like being different from everyone else. I was nervous, too, because I thought even the teachers at Lindamood-Bell might not be able to help me.

But much to my surprise, I *liked* being tutored! The teachers were so nice, and patient, too—no one ever got mad at me. I had five different teachers, and they all had lots of ways of explaining things. It almost seemed like they tricked my brain into understanding how to sound out words. Finally—after a long time—everything just clicked, and I could read!

> "It seemed like they tricked my brain into understanding."

EVERYONE WAS AMAZED WHEN I WENT BACK TO MY regular school. When it was my turn to read aloud, some of the kids in my class couldn't believe I was really reading. They thought maybe I'd heard the story before and memorized it! Some of the kids even said the school I'd gone to must have been really good, because I was reading so well.

I'm in third grade now, and I love reading. I usually get 100% on my spelling tests. Now I know I was never stupid—I just needed some extra help.

8-10% of kids under 18 have some type of learning disability.

(NIH.gov)

"I have pricked my fingers more than 16,000 times to test my blood sugar."

Diabetes Changed My Whole Life

By Caroline, age 11, Tex.

I WAS FIVE WHEN I WAS DIAGNOSED WITH diabetes. I'd always been a skinny kid, but in two weeks, I'd lost seven pounds. I was thirsty all the time, even though I kept drinking tons of water. On top of that, I had to pee every 45 minutes, even in the middle of the night.

My mom was shocked when the doctor said I had diabetes. She didn't think you could get diabetes unless someone else in your family had it, too. But most people who get juvenile diabetes—the kind I have—don't have someone else in their family with the disease. No one knows for sure what causes it.

"My mom was shocked when the doctor said I had diabetes."

Learning about Diabetes

So what is diabetes? Everyone has an organ called a pancreas. The pancreas secretes something called insulin, which your body needs to turn the sugar in your food (even food that isn't sweet, like milk and vegetables) into energy. When you have diabetes, your pancreas doesn't produce insulin. Without it, you can end up with too much sugar in your blood, which makes you feel really sick.

Because my body doesn't make any insulin, I have to take insulin every day to control my blood sugar. With too little insulin, you get high blood sugar, which can make you go into a coma, have kidney failure, and die. But if you get too much insulin, your blood sugar can go too low, and that's just as dangerous.

"If my blood sugar goes too low, I feel dizzy and weak."

Finger Pricks

To make sure I get the right amount of insulin, I have to check my blood sugar 8 to 10 times a day, including before I eat anything, exercise, or go anywhere. I prick my finger and squeeze out a drop of blood onto a little machine called a glucometer. If my blood sugar is too high, I have to give myself insulin, and if it is too low, sugar.

I used to get insulin from shots I would give myself. Now I have an insulin pump that is attached to a tube or "catheter," which is inserted in my body 24-7. The pump, which is about the size of a small cell phone, attaches to my shorts or skirt. The pump drips insulin into my body every three minutes, trying to act like a normal pancreas. I can also tell it to give me insulin whenever my blood sugar goes too high, or when I am eating. The pump makes my life easier, but it is not a cure.

Blood Sugar Woes

Since the day of my diagnosis, I have pricked my fingers more than 16,000 times to test my blood sugar. I've had over 7,000 injections of insulin and 250 catheter insertions. If my blood sugar goes too low, I feel dizzy and weak. If my blood sugar goes too high, I get extremely thirsty and have to pee a lot. I never know how I'm going to feel during the day or night, and sometimes I go for days without feeling "good."

Probably the worst thing about having diabetes is worrying about what it might do to me. The disease can cause complications, like kidney damage, blindness, or heart disease. I used to think that if I took really good care of myself I wouldn't get complications. But I am already beginning to have kidney problems. I try not to think about it, but when I'm alone it is sometimes all I *can* think about.

"Diabetes makes me different from other kids, and sometimes that's very hard."

What I Can Do...

I have learned some things from having diabetes, though. I know that I am responsible enough to take care of my body. It is really hard work to keep my blood sugar at the right level, but I do everything I can to keep it balanced.

There is also some good that has come from me having diabetes, as strange as that sounds. I've discovered that I can do something to make a difference in the world. Scientists are working very hard to find a cure for diabetes, but the research is expensive. For several years, my family has worked to raise money for the Juvenile Diabetes Research Foundation (the JDRF). A few years ago, I decided I wanted to do even more.

I Testified Before Congress

When I was nine, I won a contest to go to the very first JDRF Children's Congress, and I spent three days in Washington, D.C. with 99 other children who had diabetes. We asked the U.S. Congress firsthand for help in finding a cure. I also testified before the U.S. Senate. These experiences showed me that I do have a voice in our government, and that people are listening.

IF I COULD STOP HAVING DIABETES TOMORROW, I'D JUMP at the chance. Every time I pass a fountain, I toss a penny in and wish for a cure. Every night I pray for a cure as long as I can stay awake. Until that day comes, though, I'll keep speaking out, and I'll keep working to raise money for research. That way, when there is a cure, I won't just be one of those who will benefit from it...I'll be one of the people who made it happen.

About 1 in every **400** kids has diabetes.
(American Diabetes Association)

I Felt So Dumb!

By Meredith, age 12, Conn.

*E*VERY NIGHT IT WAS THE SAME THING. My parents would try to help me with my homework, but before long they'd be mad at me and I'd be in tears...again.

"What's the answer, Mere? Come on, you have to try! You'll never finish this homework unless you try harder!" I could hear how frustrated my mom was. It was always like that.

She wasn't the only one who was mad. I was too, because I was trying—I always tried. But that didn't seem to matter. No matter how hard I tried, I couldn't work fast enough. It was impossible to concentrate. Sometimes, even if I could see the answer in my head, I couldn't say it or write it down right. I took way too long to finish problems. Math, especially, was a nightmare.

> "I still couldn't concentrate, and I was always disorganized."

ADHD

Maybe you've heard of ADD (Attention Deficit Disorder). It's also called ADHD (Attention Deficit Hyperactivity Disorder), and there's probably at least one kid in your class who has it.

I was diagnosed in second grade. Sitting in the doctor's office, it was a relief to hear there was a name for what was wrong with me. I knew I had a problem. I had so much more trouble in school than everyone else. Other kids finished their work-sheets in class, but my folders were full of half-done papers. My printing was terrible. I constantly forgot things. I was a little scared about what the doctor was saying, but mostly I was relieved. Now, I thought, he'd tell my mom and dad how to fix me.

Three years later, I was in fourth grade and *still* strug-gling with school. Even though I was taking medication and my parents were trying to help me, things weren't going very well. I still couldn't concentrate, and I was always disorganized. It took me forever to finish assignments. I was still forgetting things—my papers, pencils, lunch tickets, permission slips, library books…if I needed it, I forgot it. My teacher yelled at me *all* the time. I came home crying almost every day.

"I could see the frustration on their faces when I couldn't get the right answer."

Too Stupid to Learn?

The worst part was that I felt so stupid. My parents and teach-ers never said I was dumb, but I could see the frustration on their faces when I couldn't get the right answer. My mom was always having conflicts with the teacher and the principal over the help I was getting in school. I wondered what was wrong me, that I was causing so much trouble. Deep down, I thought I must just be too stupid to learn. I felt so bad about myself, and so alone.

Other kids thought I was stupid, too. They made fun of me for being dumb. If I tried to laugh off my problems by calling *myself* dumb, they accused me of faking it just to get attention. I couldn't win. I acted as if I didn't care, but it really hurt.

"But the biggest surprise from the testing was that I'm gifted!"

Retested

Finally, at the end of fourth grade, the school decided that I needed to be tested some more. Getting tested was a good thing for me, because it convinced my parents that all my incomplete assignments weren't due to laziness or a bad attitude. My brain just couldn't stay focused long enough to finish them.

The tests told us other things too, like that I can't process information if it's presented in certain ways. For example, if my teacher wrote 10 vocabulary words on the board and said the class had to write them down and memorize them, I'd probably get an F. But if I can learn the same words by having someone speak them to me, I'll do fine.

Gifted!

But the biggest surprise from the testing was that I'm gifted! After thinking I was dumb for so long, I couldn't believe it when they told me.

It's not as if school suddenly got easy after that, but it *did* slowly start to change. I was accepted into Summit, our school's program for gifted and talented students. I got to be a lot more creative—and that's one thing I can really shine at. I started to like school, or at least some parts of it. I was still in the lowest math group and that still made me feel dumb, but… well, math isn't *everything*, and at least I knew why.

This year, things have gotten so much better. I'm going to a private school, where there are more kids—*cool* kids, even—who have ADD. I have great friends, and I don't feel alone anymore. I have a therapist who helps me with strategies for school problems, and a tutor who helps me organize and prioritize my work. We've even finally figured out my medication.

I KNOW NOW THAT I'M NOT DUMB, AND I DON'T HATE MY ADD anymore. Even though it's caused me tons of trouble, there's a good side to it too. Having a brain that's wired a little differently from most people's means that I see things differently. And that can be a really good thing, especially when you're trying to solve a problem or a mystery or just be creative. So maybe my brain is a little weird…that just makes me unique! ADD is part of me, and these days, I'm happy just the way I am.

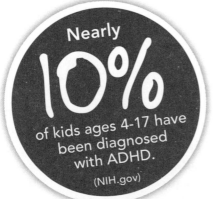

Nearly **10%** of kids ages 4-17 have been diagnosed with ADHD. (NIH.gov)

Find out more about ADHD/ADD! →

What Is ADHD/ADD?

ADHD stands for Attention Deficit Hyperactivity Disorder, a condition that makes it really hard to sit still and/or concentrate. It's also sometimes called ADD. Having ADHD is sort of like being nearsighted and needing glasses, except it's your brain that needs help focusing. The things people use to focus the brain—organizational tools, exercise, and even medication—are kind of like glasses for your brain. Some people with ADHD are more "nearsighted" than others, so they need more tools, just like some people need stronger glasses.

What Are the Symptoms?

There are three basic types of ADHD. The symptoms are:

Hyperactive type
▶ Can't sit still—fidgets, jumps up, wiggles in seat.
▶ Talks too much, interrupts conversations.
▶ Does or says things without thinking about the consequences.
▶ Finds it very hard to take turns or wait.

Inattentive type
▶ Has trouble concentrating, is easily distracted or bored.
▶ Doesn't pay attention to details; makes a lot of careless mistakes.
▶ Often forgets assignments, books, papers.
▶ Has trouble finishing work.
▶ May seem spacey or daydream a lot.

Combined hyperactive/inattentive type
▶ Shows signs of both hyperactive and inattentive types.

Everyone shows some of these symptoms some of the time. The symptoms are only considered a problem when they go on for a long time and occur more often than in other kids your age.

Who Gets ADHD?

About nine kids out of 100 have ADHD. In a class of 30 kids, there's usually one who has it. More boys have ADHD than girls, but it affects both.

What Causes ADHD?

No one knows for sure, but if your parents have it, you're more likely to have it, too. Some scientists think it's caused by low levels of certain chemicals in the brain. Whatever the cause may be, ADHD is never anyone's fault, and you can't make it go away just by trying harder.

Treatment

Since symptoms can be very different from one person to the next, treatments also vary a great deal. However, if you're diagnosed with ADHD, you'll probably receive counseling and may be given medication. Since many kids who have ADHD also have learning disabilities, you may also need tutoring or extra help with school.

The Silver Lining

Can you have ADHD and still be successful? Absolutely! Some people feel that ADHD helps them to be creative, to come up with outside-the-box solutions, and even to have a laser-like focus on the things that really grab their interest. You can't get rid of ADHD, but if you learn how to deal with it, you may find that you can turn something you thought was a weakness into your greatest strength.

High achievers with ADHD:

Ty Pennington, the star of ABC's Extreme Makeover: Home Edition, was diagnosed in high school and still takes medication. Today he hosts a hit TV show, designs his own line of home décor items, and works to educate people about ADHD.

David Neeleman, founder of Jet Blue Airlines, says, "If someone told me you could be normal or you could continue to have your ADD, I would take ADD. Along with the disorganization, procrastination, [and] inability to focus…there also comes creativity and the ability to take risks."

Michael Phelps, swimmer and Olympic gold medalist, was diagnosed at age 9. Michael chose not to be treated with medication and instead found that swimming helped release his extra energy and gave him the discipline he needed to excel.

How to Deal

Everyone has trouble concentrating sometimes! People with ADHD just have more trouble than most. If you've never been tested for ADHD but think you might have it, talk to your parents or teacher about the way you feel. They can help you understand whether your symptoms are really due to ADHD or are just the normal concentration problems everyone experiences.

If you have been diagnosed with ADHD, your parents, doctor, and teachers should be working to get you the help you need, but there's also a lot you can do to help yourself. Here's a good place to start.

Just about anyone can benefit from doing these things, but they're especially important if you have ADHD.

✔ **Sit up front.** If you can, find a seat at the front of the class, so you won't have as many distractions.

✔ **Unplug.** Turn off e-mail, IM, and your phone (if you have one) when you're doing homework or other tasks that require your full attention, so that you don't become distracted.

✔ **Write it down.** Keep a homework notebook or pocket calendar with all your assignments and their due dates written down in one place.

✔ **Check your work.** If you tend to make careless mistakes, it's especially important that you double-check all your assignments before you turn them in.

✔ **Exercise.** Some studies have shown that exercise helps people who have ADHD. If you're hyperactive, it's particularly helpful to burn off all that excess energy. When you're doing homework, take short breaks to run around outside. You'll focus better afterwards.

More Info, Please

Need more information? Check out these resources:

Kidshealth.org: To go straight to their articles on ADHD, click on "Kids Site" and then search on "ADHD." You might want to read the articles on learning disabilities, too.

Attention, Girls! A Guide to Learn All About Your AD/HD by Patricia Quinn (Magination Press): This book explains everything, and best of all, it's especially for girls!

Why Are Friendships So Confusing?

SHE KNOWS EVERYTHING about you...she'd never tell your secrets...she's your biggest fan. Who doesn't want a friend like that?

True friendship is a gift... but it can be hard to find. Whether you're stuck in a fading friendship, caught in the popularity trap, or dealing with mean girls, we'll break down the solutions to your problems step by step. Best of all, we'll teach you how to free yourself from poisonous friendships forever and be the best friend you can be.

Soon, you'll be meeting new people and making friends who truly respect and understand you...because you deserve first-rate friendships.

When Did Life Get So Complicated?

Sᴛᴜᴄᴋ ʙᴇᴛᴡᴇᴇɴ ꜰʀɪᴇɴᴅꜱ? Tired of your siblings? Self-conscious about your body? Crushing big time?

You're not alone. Every month, girls write to *Discovery Girls* magazine to ask Ali, our advice columnist, for help with issues like these.

When it comes to girls' most troublesome questions, Ali has all the answers you need. She tackles your questions on everything from family to friendship to school to boys...and much, much more.

No matter what you're going through, you'll find answers to your problems inside. Ali is here to help!

Getting Unstuck

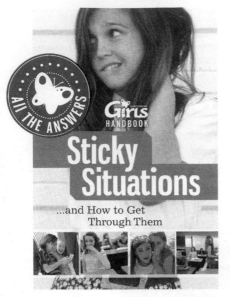

Girls HANDBOOK

Sticky Situations

...and How to Get Through Them

Remember when you got up the courage to tell your crush you liked him...and found out he didn't like you back? Didn't you wish you knew someone who had all the answers?

Well, have no fear! Not only do we know exactly how to handle your crush (what is wrong with him, anyway?), but we also know how to deal with a gazillion other sticky situations. Like when your BFF blabs your deepest secret to the entire school...or when you make a total fool of yourself onstage.

We'll also tell you how to handle being bullied by mean girls... or stranded at the mall...and much, much more! By the last page, you'll be ready to deal with anything!